Chapter 1

Sir Nick the Brave gripped his sword
and advanced on the Black Knight.
"Prepare to fight!" he shouted, charging.

The Black Knight threw his sword down.
"I don't want to play knights again,"
he said. "We played it yesterday and the
day before and…well, it's boring."

Sir Nick stopped and pushed his visor up. He glared at the Black Knight. Or rather, his friend Oliver. "It's not a game," said Nick. "It's training for when I become a *real* knight."

"No one becomes a knight nowadays,"
said Oliver. "Can't we play football?
There's an important match tomorrow."

"Tea's ready!" said the Black Knight's mum.

"Gadzooks! We'll call it a draw,"
said Nick.

Chapter 2

"What did you two do at school today?"

asked Oliver's mum at tea.

"I played football," said Oliver. "I scored

seven goals."

"That's my boy!" said Oliver's dad.

Nick tried not to yawn. Football was so boring! It would be much better if there were swords and lances and dragons involved…

"Are you playing in the match tomorrow, Nick?" asked Oliver's dad.

Nick shook his head. "I don't think so."

"Nick's not interested in football," said Oliver. "He just wants to be a knight."

"A knight? Well, I'm sure there'll be a bit of jousting going on. It is a tournament, after all!" chuckled Oliver's dad. Nick's eyes widened. A tournament? With knights and jousting and stuff? This could be his big chance!

He let his visor fall back down and
imagined himself galloping across a field,
holding his lance ready to lock his enemy
in battle, cheered on by admiring crowds...
"Do you want pudding, Nick? NICK!"

Chapter 3

In school the next day, Oliver and Nick
raced to the sports hall noticeboard. On it
was the match line-up. Oliver pointed.

"Nick – you're on the bench!" he exclaimed.

"What does that mean?" Nick asked.

"You're a sub. You come on if someone's injured," Oliver explained. Nick was disappointed. He really wanted to do some jousting!

They went into the changing room. Nick
started polishing his armour and put his
helmet on. The other players all laughed.
"You can't wear armour!" said Oliver.
"Why not?" asked Nick. "In a tournament
all the knights wear armour."

Just then the coach came in. He didn't see

Nick, who was facing the other way.

"Ready everyone? Let's play some football!"

Chapter 4

Oliver and the team marched out onto the pitch. Nick found the bench and sat down next to the other subs, clutching his lance. There was a loud whistle. The tournament had begun!

Nick tried to lift his visor to see what was happening, but it was stuck fast. Suddenly there was a roar from the crowd.

"What's happening?" Nick asked the sub next to him.

"Our goalie was fouled. He's coming off!" the boy exclaimed.

There was another roar.

"What now?" asked Nick. He fiddled

with his visor, but it wouldn't budge.

"The other team scored," said the boy.

He jumped up. "I'm on!" he shouted,

and ran onto the pitch.

The other team scored again and again. And they played dirty. Two more players from Nick's team were fouled and had to come off. Four nil...PHWEEEEEEEEEEEEP! The half-time whistle went. Nick called out only to find he was the last person left on the bench!

Chapter 5

In the break, Nick found Oliver in the

changing room. "They play really rough,"

moaned Oliver. "We haven't got a chance."

"Do you want to borrow my armour?"

asked Nick. Oliver shook his head.

They trudged back out to the pitch.

PHWEEEEEEEEEEEEEP! The game started.

A minute later, there was a scream. A mean-looking defender had slammed into one of Nick's team. Another man down! Nick heard the coach shouting at him. His heart jumped. He was on! He raised his lance and charged onto the pitch.

"ON GUARD, SCURVY DOGS!" he roared. The crowd gasped! The other team froze in astonishment. Nick thundered down the pitch, waving his lance.

He couldn't see the ball. In fact, he couldn't see much at all. Then his lance hit something. THWUMP! The ball sliced off and whacked one of the enemy on the head.

The enemy fell over. "Foul!" he shouted.

The ref looked frantically in his rule book,

but it didn't say anything about lances.

He shook his head. No foul.

"DIM-WITTED DOLTS!" yelled Nick,

charging up the pitch in the opposite

direction to the ball.

Two confused defenders tried to stop him, but he swerved aside and they bashed headfirst into each other. It was chaos!

Oliver suddenly leapt into action.

He found the ball, ran with it, shot –

"GOAAAAAAAAAAAAAAAAAAAAAL!"

Oliver scored again! And again! The other team were falling to pieces, with half of them chasing Nick around the pitch.

Two…three…four goals! They were level.
But they still needed one goal to win and
there was only one minute left to score it.
Behind his visor, Nick was sweating. It was
hard work, this jousting. He stopped. Then
he heard shouting. Three – no, four – big,
cross enemies were thundering towards him.

"NICK! THIS WAY!" Nick heard Oliver's voice. He swerved and ran blindly towards Oliver. The defenders were closing in...

THWACK! Nick's visor shot up. He saw stars. The ball had hit his helmet...it rocketed towards the goal...the goalie leapt to save it – but it was too late!

ROAAAAAAAARRRR!

The crowd jumped to their feet, cheering madly. The final whistle blew. Nick Knight had scored the winning goal!

A month later, Nick and Oliver were in the changing room. "Can you fix my visor?" Nick asked Oliver. The rest of the team were polishing their armour.

"OK, boys – are you ready?" called the
coach. Nick and Oliver grinned.

"Time to play some joustball!" said Nick.

"Gadzooks, Sir Nick, I think you're right!"
said Oliver.

Franklin Watts
First published in Great Britain in 2015 by
The Watts Publishing Group

Text © Sam Watkins 2015
Illustrations © Davide Ortu 2015

The rights of Sam Watkins to be
identified as the author and Davide Ortu
as the illustrator of this Work have been
asserted in accordance with the Copyright,
Designs and Patents Act, 1988.

Series Editor: Melanie Palmer
Series Advisor: Catherine Glavina
Cover Design: Cathryn Gilbert
Design Manager: Peter Scoulding

A CIP catalogue record for this book is
available from the British Library.

ISBN 978 1 4451 4286 9 (hbk)
ISBN 978 1 4451 4287 6 (pbk)
ISBN 978 1 4451 4288 3 (library ebook)

Printed in China

Franklin Watts
An imprint of
Hachette Children's Group
Part of The Watts Publishing Group
Carmelite House
50 Victoria Embankment
London EC4Y 0DZ

An Hachette UK Company
www.hachette.co.uk

www.franklinwatts.co.uk

MIX
Paper from
responsible sources
FSC® C104740
FSC
www.fsc.org